SHEBA
THE GOOD MUSLIM CAT

This book belongs to:

_____

Published by Tughra Books
335 Clifton Ave.
Clifton, NJ, 07011, USA
www.tughrabooks.com

Library of Congress Cataloging-in-Publication Data

Names: Elfarrah, Carima, author. | Yusuf, Aaron, illustrator.
Title: Sheba : the good Muslim cat / by Carima Elfarrah ; illustrated by Aaron Yusuf.
Description: Clifton : Tughra Books, 2024. | Audience: Ages 4-8 | Audience: Grades K-1
Identifiers: LCCN 2023045883 (print) | LCCN 2023045884 (ebook) | ISBN 9781597849616 (hardcover) | ISBN 9781597849968 (ebook)
Subjects: LCSH: Household animals--Juvenile literature. | Household animals--Religious aspects--Islam. | Pets--Juvenile literature. | Pets--Religious aspects--Islam.
Classification: LCC QL49 .E4115 2024 (print) | LCC QL49 (ebook) | DDC 636--dc23/eng/20231102
LC record available at https://lccn.loc.gov/2023045883
LC ebook record available at https://lccn.loc.gov/2023045884

SHEBA
The Good Muslim Cat

by
Carima Elfarrah

Illustrated by
Aaron Yusuf

My family has an extraordinary pet.

Her name is Sheba, and she's more than you'd expect.

Her blue eyes shine like the rarest sapphire.

Of her loving company, we never tire.

But that's not what makes her special, you see.

Our family is Muslim, and so is she!

Meow

A Muslim cat!? How can that be!?

Puurr
Puurr
Puurr

In the early morning, my daddy reads Qur'an.
She lingers near him as if she could understand,

That this blessed book is something GRAND!
She purrs and rubs against his hand.

14 When salah time comes, we all take ou
And she always comes running, as if it's a

She stays beside us until we say the last "salaam."
And then she pounces and plays with the imam.

If ever her water or food bowls are empty,
She sits beside them, waiting patiently.

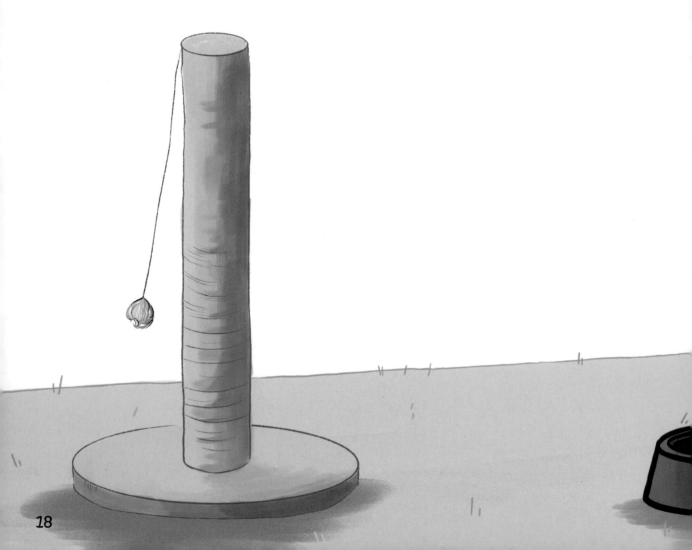

She never whines or makes a fuss.
She's better than the rest of us!

My mama says she hopes we'd be,
More like that well-mannered kitty.

Of all the places she could sleep,
At night, she curls up at my feet.

And every morning, at fajr she cries
And makes sure for the prayer we arise.

My mama told me that the Blessed Prophet ﷺ said,
And it often echoes in my head:

"Allah rewards every act that's admirable,
Even kindness done to an animal."

We are grateful to Allah for our furry feline friend.
Because of her, opportunities for rewards never end!

And we hope, one day she might attest,
Before Allah, that we did our best.

This story is inspired by Shiekh Shukari,
a Wali (friend) of Allah and scholar of Damascus, Syria.

Shiekh Shukari was very poor and yet every day he would
share his food with two cats that would visit him in his patio.
One day, only one cat arrived at mealtime.
He wondered aboud what had happened to the other cat
and placed the plate of food before the solitary cat, encouraging him to eat.
The cat looked him straight in his eyes and said, "By Allah, I will not eat.
I have only come to tell you my friend has died and before he died,
he asked me to tell you that when he meets Allah;
he will attest to your kindness and generosity.
And imagine, if that is how you have been with us, while we are cats,
how your Lord will be with you."

In other words, no kindness done to any living being
will ever be overlooked by Allah, the most High.
We should never belittle any act of kindness,
rather we should strive to do as much good as
we can and be hopeful of the rewards that await.
If we intend His pleasure, we will find our reward with Him.

He is the Most Generous and the Most Kind.

Glossary

Muslim- is an Arabic word that means, "one who is in submission," it refers to followers of the religion of Islam.

Allah- is an Arabic word that means, "the God," it refers to the One Creator and Originator of everything created. Allah is the proper name of God. Allah has no gender, no plural, and no image.

Qur'an- is an Arabic word that means, "recitation." It refers to the revealed book of the Muslims. It is understood to be the word-for-word speech of Allah, and it has been preserved exactly as it was revealed over 1400 years ago. Muslims believe reciting the Qur'an brings blessings and protection to one's life and home.

Salah- is an Arabic word that means, "prayer." It is derived from the Arabic root word "Silah," which means, "connection." Implying that the prayer is our connection to Allah, the most High. In Islam, Muslims pray at least five times a day. Salah is the second of the five pillars of Islam. [1. Testimony of Faith 2. Five times a day prayer 3. Fasting the month of Ramadan. 4. Charity 5. Performance of Hajj (pilgrimage to Mecca), at least once in a lifetime, if one is able (financially and physically.)]

Salaam- is the Arabic word that means, "peace." It is the beginning of the salutation that Muslims greet each other with, "As-salaamu alaykum," meaning: "peace be upon you all." It is also the prescribed way of ending the ritual prayer, by turning one's head to the right and then the left while pronouncing, "As-salaamu alaykum."

Imam- is the Arabic word that means "leader." It refers to the one who leads the ritual prayer. A woman may be the imam for other women, and a child may be the imam for other children.

Fajr- is the Arabic word for "dawn." It refers to the ritual prayer made before the rising of the sun.

ﷺ- These Arabic words read, "Sallallahu alayhi wa salaam." It is the expression used to send blessings on the Prophet Muhammad. It means, "Allah bless him and give him peace."

Muslims use this expression to make reverence for the Prophet Muhammad every time his name is mentioned. Doing this is an etiquette he himself taught us. It is a way of expressing love for him, and a means for reward from Allah Most High, for honoring His Beloved Prophet. ﷺ

About the Book

Sheba, the Good Muslim Cat is a picture book in rhyme about a Muslim family with a pious cat! Sheba participates in and seems to enjoy the various religious practices the family engages in throughout the day. The story invites young readers to consider the tremendous blessing and benefit a family pet can provide them in this life and the next. The true account of a scholar whose pet cat once spoke to him, makes the story even more transcendent and magnificent! The simple act of loving and taking care of one›s family cat is in reality a glorious opportunity to draw closer to Allah. This story will inspire and delight even the smallest readers who might have always felt a spiritual connection with their family pet.

About the Author

Carima Elfarrah lives in Melilla, Spain, with her husband, five children, and their good Muslim cat Sheba. She is the founder and director of an Islamic nonprofit association: Songs of Paradise. In addition to directing a girls' choir, she develops and teaches educational and artistic programs for Muslim children of all ages.